Louis Armstrong

Jazz Musician

Patricia and Fredrick McKissack

Illustrated by Ned O.

❖ *Great African Americans Series* ❖

Enslow Publishers, Inc.

40 Industrial Road   PO Box 38

Box 398   Aldershot

Berkeley Heights, NJ 07922   Hants GU12 6BP

USA   UK

http://www.enslow.com

To Robert Carwell, Sr.
A special thanks to our friends at the Missouri Historical Society in
St. Louis

Library of Congress Cataloging-in-Publication Data

McKissack, Pat 1944–
      Louis Armstrong: jazz musician / Patricia and Fredrick McKissack;
illustrated by Ned O.
            p. cm. — (Great African Americans series)
      Includes index.
      Summary: Simple text and illustrations describe the life and
accomplishments of the jazz trumpeter who was nicknamed Satchmo.
      ISBN 0-89490-307-1
      1. Armstrong, Louis, 1900–1971—Juvenile literature. 2. Jazz
musicians—United States—Biography—Juvenile literature.
[1. Armstrong, Louis, 1900–1971. 2. Musicians. 3. Jazz. 4. Afro-
Americans—Biography.] I. McKissack, Fredrick. II. Ostendorf,
Edward, ill. III. Title. IV. Series: McKissack, Pat, 1944– Great
African Americans series.
ML3930.A75M4   1991
781.65'092—dc20
[B]   91-12420
                                                            CIP
                                                           AC MN
Printed in the United States of America
10 9 8 7 6
Photo credits: Frank Driggs Collection, p. 14; Library of Congress, p. 4; Missouri
Historical Society, Hangge photo, p. 6; Missouri Historical Society, Block Brothers
photo, p. 12; Moorland-Spingarn Research Center, Howard University, pp. 16, 19,
21, 28; Copyright *Washington Post*; Reprinted by permission of the D.C. Public
Library, pp. 22, 25, 26, 27; William Ransom Hogan Jazz Archive, Tulane University
Library, p. 10.
Illustration credits: Ned O., pp. 7, 8, 11, 15, 18, 20, 24.
Cover illustration: Ned O.

Contents

Louis Armstrong
Born: July 4, 1900, New Orleans, Louisiana.
Died: July 6, 1971, Corona, New York.

1

Off to a Bad Start

In 1900 New Orleans, Louisiana, was a busy city. One of the places people liked to go for a good time was Black Storyville.

Black Storyville had lots of bars and **dance halls**.* There were lots of fights. This is where Louis Armstrong was born on July 4, 1900.

Louis's family was very poor. They

---

* Words in **bold type** are explained in *Words to Know* on page 30.

lived in a one-room shack. His mother, Maryann, did different jobs. Grandmama Josephine took care of Louis and his little sister, Mama Lucy. His father was not around very much.

Black Storyville was full of crime. But something very special was happening there. A new kind of music was being played. It was called **jazz**.

Louis loved the sound of Storyville jazz. It was a part of him. No other music was like jazz. It was special.

People loved jazz. It was happy music. It was played on river-boats that took people down the Mississippi River to New Orleans.

Grandmama Josephine took Louis and his sister to church almost every Sunday. Louis enjoyed singing the old **spirituals**. Those old songs were special to him, too.

Louis hated school and wouldn't go. Instead he sold papers on the street. He used the money to help buy food for his family.

"You're going to end up in trouble," Grandmama Josephine always warned Louis. And she was right.

2

In Trouble

Louis and three of his friends started a singing group. They sang on street corners for money.

One day Louis found a gun in an old trunk. He waited until New Year's Eve. Then he shot the gun. His friends laughed and cheered. Then Louis pointed the gun at a boy who had been bothering him and his friends . . . and pulled the trigger.

Suddenly a policeman took hold of Louis. The bullets were not real. No one was really hurt. Louis was just trying to scare the bully.

But the **judge** didn't see it that way. Louis was sent to **reform school**.

Louis was twelve years old. " I thought the world was coming to an end," he said later.

Many years later, Louis and his band (front row) came back to visit the reform school. The school still had a band. Mr. Peter Davis (standing right) was still teaching music.

Peter Davis taught music at the school. He asked Louis to play the **cornet**. Louis joined the **brass band**. By the end of the year, he was leading the band.

Once Louis led the band through Storyville. His family cheered. So did his friends. It was a day Louis never forgot.

Louis stayed in reform school for two years. "Being there saved my life," he said years later.

Dixieland Jazz was a new and exciting kind of music. It was first played in New Orleans, and then spread up the Mississippi River to St. Louis. The Cotton Club Band from St. Louis was a famous band in the early 1900s.

3

And All That Jazz

Louis was sent to live with his father. But before long, he was back with Grandmama Josephine in Black Storyville.

He took a job selling papers. With his first check, he bought a horn. Then he started playing with jazz bands in Storyville bars. He worked all day and played his horn at night.

In 1917 many black jazz **musicians** went to Chicago and New York to play. One great **trumpeter** was Joe Oliver. He liked Louis. Louis thought Oliver was the best trumpeter.

When Oliver left for Chicago, Louis was asked to take his seat in the Kid Ory Band. At last Louis got a chance to be heard.

Soon people were coming to Black Storyville just to hear Louis Armstrong.

Louis worked on a riverboat during the summer of 1919. He washed dishes and also played in the band (third from right).

Joe Oliver asked Louis to come play the cornet in Chicago. So he went. There he married Lil Hardin. She played the piano.

Lil wanted Louis to start his own band. But Louis wasn't ready. He played with some of the best bands in New York and Chicago.

In the 1920s everyone was talking about jazz . . . jazz . . . and more jazz. And the jazz player most people were talking about was Louis Armstrong.

Louis's first marriage failed. Then he married Lillian Hardin in 1924. She had gone to Fisk University in Nashville, Tennessee. She played jazz piano in the King Oliver Band.

4

Oh, Yeaaaaah!

For many years Louis played the cornet.
One night he played the **trumpet**. It was
larger than the cornet. He liked its sound.
From then on he played the trumpet.

Louis also made records with many
different bands. More and more people
heard his music. He made them love the
sounds of Storyville jazz the same way he
did. "It's a hot sound," he said. Then he
would wipe his face with a big, white
handkerchief.

At last Louis started his own band. They went all over the United States playing jazz . . . jazz . . . and more jazz.

Sometimes when Louis played he also sang. His voice sounded like he had a bad cold. But that was his own special sound.

There is a story people tell about Louis Armstrong. It may or may not be true. It is

In 1929 Louis was in *Hot Chocolates*, a Broadway musical. He also made several hit records.

said that one night he was singing and forgot the words. So he made trumpet sounds with his voice. Do-skid-dat-de-dat-dat-do. That way of singing is called **scatting**.

And at the end of a song, Louis always sang "Oh, yeaaaaah!" People waited so that they could join him in singing, "Oh, yeaaaaah!"

Louis worked very hard to please a crowd. "Music makes me happy," he always told his audiences. "I want to make you happy, too." And he did.

Louis played with many famous musicians. Gene Krupa was
a well-known drummer.

5

Satchmo

Louis had not taken his band to New Orleans. So in 1931 he went back to his home city.

His mother, Maryann, died in 1927. But the rest of his family came to hear his band play.

Some people in the South thought black and white musicians should not play together in the same band. Louis thought differently. His band had members of different races. So Louis and his band were

turned away from some hotels. They were called names. But his band stayed together and played great music. Lots of people came to hear them. They enjoyed the music.

Louis's friends called him "**Satchel Mouth**," because his smile was so big. (A satchel is a suitcase that opens wide.) Over the years "Satchel Mouth" became "Satchmo." By the late 1930s everybody was calling Louis Armstrong "Satchmo." And he loved it.

Louis never forgot his early life. He often played at prisons.

Louis and Lil were no longer together. There were always large crowds around him. But Satchmo was lonely. His music was sad. Then he married Lucille Wilson, a beautiful dancer. Satchmo was happy again. So was his music.

President Richard Nixon named Armstrong a **goodwill ambassador**.

Louis played his music all over the world. Here he is with his wife Lucille Wilson (left) in Japan. They were met by a famous Japanese singer (middle.)

Louis sang to kings and queens and world leaders. Here he is playing at the birthday of President Franklin D. Roosevelt.

Satchmo won many awards. He was in the well-known movie
Hello Dolly in 1969. The title song was one of his best selling
records.

Louis went all over the world playing music and making friends.

Satchmo made many records. He was in several movies. He had one big hit song: "Hello Dolly." It sold millions of copies. He also won many **awards**. He never wanted to stop playing music.

And he never did. He lived and made music until he was 71 years old.

He died on July 6, 1971.

Words to Know

award—An honor given to a person who has done something special.

brass band—A group of musicians who play one of the brass horns: trombone, tuba, French horn, trumpet, or cornet.

cornet—A brass horn; a musical instrument.

dance hall—A place where people go to dance.

goodwill ambassador—A person who represents the United States around the world.

handkerchief—Square piece of cloth used by people to wipe their face, hands, or noses.

jazz—A special type of music developed in the early 1900s.

judge—The person who decides a court case.

musicians (myoo-ZISH-uhns)—People who play instruments and make music.

reform school—A special school where children who get into trouble with the law are sent.

"Satchel Mouth"—A playful name for a person with a very large mouth. A satchel is a kind of suitcase that opens wide.

scatting—A kind of singing without using words. A person's voice is used to make sounds like an instrument.

spirituals—Religious songs that were first sung by African-American slaves.

trumpet—A brass horn; a musical instrument.

trumpeter—A person who plays the trumpet.

Index

JBN ARMSTRONG M
MCKISSACK, PATRICIA.
LOUIS ARMONSTRONG: JAZZ MUSICIAN.

FREEPORT MEMORIAL LIBRARY
FREEPORT, NEW YORK
PHONE: 379-3274

GAYLORD M